Little RIDDLERS

Southern England

Edited By Donna Samworth

First published in Great Britain in 2018 by:

YoungWriters

Young Writers
Remus House
Coltsfoot Drive
Peterborough
PE2 9BF
Telephone: 01733 890066
Website: www.youngwriters.co.uk

Book Design by Ashley Janson

SB ISBN 978-1-78896-625-2
Printed and bound in the UK by BookPrintingUK
Website: www.bookprintinguk.com
YB0364R

FOREWORD

Dear Reader,

Are you ready to get your thinking caps on to puzzle your way through this wonderful collection?

Young Writers' Little Riddlers competition set out to encourage young writers to create their own riddles. Their answers could be whatever or whoever their imaginations desired; from people to places, animals to objects, food to seasons. Riddles are a great way to further the children's use of poetic expression, including onomatopoeia and similes, as well as encourage them to 'think outside the box' by providing clues without giving the answer away immediately.

All of us here at Young Writers believe in the importance of inspiring young children to produce creative writing, including poetry, and we feel that seeing their own riddles in print will keep that creative spirit burning brightly and proudly.

We hope you enjoy riddling your way through this book as much as we enjoyed reading all the entries.

CONTENTS

St Martin's Garden Primary School, Odd Down

Lola Williams (7)	114
Taheena Chowdhury (7)	115
Jacob David Lewis (6)	116
Aimee Schofield (7)	117
Erin Sherwood (6)	118
Ashton Morrissey-Hoskin (7)	119
Kyle Martin (7)	120
Heather Jade Bean (7)	121
Jakub Chelstowski (7)	122
Nyah Quinnell-Reid (7)	123
Natalie Pranczuk-Doubrouska (7)	124
Ashley Powell (7)	125
Jack White (6)	126
Wojciech Cejrowski (6)	127
Summer Lewis (6)	128
Leland Jones (6)	129
Leon Ricketts (6)	130

Stoke Park Primary School, Lockleaze

Brooke Franklin (7)	131
Bayley Drew (6)	132
Archie Neale (7)	133
Harvey Mark Bee's (6)	134
Evie Butt (6)	135
Mohammed Elsadig Yagoeb (6)	136
Taija Louise Allen (6)	137
Hassan Omar (7)	138
Ryan Collins (6)	139
Milosz Siecinski (7)	140
Layla Toogood (6)	141
Minnie Jamelia Manu Edkins (7)	142
Micah Ogbu (7)	143
Elly Underwood (6)	144
Brianne Georgina Bond (6)	145
Filip Nogawka (6)	146

The Ursuline Preparatory School, Ilford

Vihaan Saraiya (7)	147
Ezaan Shaikh (6)	148
Swayam Sinha (6)	149
Aniyah Akram (6)	150
Shemilore Aderugbo (7)	151
Kayla Olatunji (6)	152
Kayla Gadiagellan (6)	153
Larelle Amanda Burnett (7)	154
Tiffany Marria Azumah (6)	155

THE POEMS

We Can Zoom

It can zoom, but it can't go up to the moon.
If you have to ask why, it's because it can hardly fly.
Although, if we hit a bump we can make it jump.
It has got tyres, it can't get a flat.
When I'm on it, I always wear a hard hat.
Two wheels are good enough for me, but my baby sister has to have three.
If we are careful we take it on the road.
But it doesn't have a hooter.
Can you guess what it is called? It is my favourite.
What is it?

Answer: A scooter.

Amie Brooks (7)
Broadhempston Primary School, Broadhempston Village

Tiny Gastropod

I am slimy.
I am very slow.
I am crunchy on the outside and squishy on the inside.
I can peek around corners with my long, thin antennae.
I hide in my shell when I get scared.
I taste good with garlic.
When you touch my eyes I pull my antennae in.
What am I?

Answer: A snail.

Max Fearon (7)
Broadhempston Primary School, Broadhempston Village

The King Of Pets

He has a long, ginger, striped tail.
He will leave a muddy trail.
He can see very well at night.
But he can disappear from sight.
He can't stay around and play.
He has to sleep by night and day.
Who is he?

Answer: Flapjack.

Violet Elizabeth Lovell (7)
Broadhempston Primary School, Broadhempston Village

What Am I?

I go pop in the microwave.
I go well with caramel.
I can come in different shapes and sizes.
I can be sweet, salty or both.
You can find me in cinemas and shops.
I am soft and crunchy.
What am I?

Answer: Popcorn.

Llewelyn Craven (7)
Broadhempston Primary School, Broadhempston Village

Prowling Through The Jungle

I have black stripes.
I live in the wild forest.
I love climbing the very tall trees.
I am a big cat.
I prowl through the long grass.
I am a lion's cousin.
What am I?

Answer: A tiger.

Ffion Salam Russell (7)
Broadhempston Primary School, Broadhempston Village

White

I am white,
Cold on the outside,
Warm on the inside,
Made in winter,
Gone in summer,
You can live inside me.
What am I?

Answer: An igloo.

Toby Mills (6)
Broadhempston Primary School, Broadhempston Village

Fluttering Happily Away

I have patches on my wings,
they can come in any colour
and I have a small antenna.
I was a caterpillar
and then I went into a cocoon and turned into...?
I can fly above a house
but it takes a long time.
I come in the spring
and I don't like the winter
because we hibernate in the winter.
When it snows we get frightened.
What am I?

Answer: A *butterfly*.

Imogen Taylor Lambert (7)
Dartmouth Academy, Dartmouth

Am I Cuddly?

I am an expert swimmer because I have webbed feet,
and I walk on my knuckles.
I lay eggs, but I'm a mammal.
I have a duck-like bill
but I can't quack or fly, but growl like a dog.
I only live in Australia.
I don't have a stomach.
I live in a burrow.
I only eat crayfish.
What am I?

Answer: A duck-billed platypus.

Lola Knott (7)

Dartmouth Academy, Dartmouth

Shelled Out

I'm oval.
I come in many sizes.
I can be many shapes when I am cooked.
I am smelly when I am in a sandwich.
I come from a farm normally.
I only come from females.
What am I?

Answer: An egg.

Maisie Louise Manning (8)
Dartmouth Academy, Dartmouth

What Is It?

It lives in the Arctic.
It looks white but is black.
It is furry.
It is the biggest mammal.
Sometimes it eats vegetables
But generally, it's a meat eater.
It looks cuddly but is pretty fearsome.
What is it?

Answer: A polar bear.

Edie Springett (7)
Georgeham CE Primary School, Georgeham

What Am I?

I can be any colour.
Wherever you go I can come with you.
I like to have shoulder rides.
I can carry lots but have no arms.
I am always behind you
but if you turn around you can't see me.
What am I?

Answer: A backpack.

Tess Matthews (7)
Georgeham CE Primary School, Georgeham

We Need Your Help

We have black skin.
We are white.
We live in the Arctic.
We eat seals.
If the ice melts we will become extinct.
We need your help.
What are we?

Answer: Polar bears.

Henry Smith (5)
Georgeham CE Primary School, Georgeham

What Am I?

What can I be?
Do I live in a tree?
Yes, I could be.
I may have sharp claws.
I may have floors in my doors.
I may live with ice in my walls.
I hunt from my prey for all of the day.
I may look like a snowman
but I'm an animal, not a man!
What am I?

Answer: Hetty the yeti.

Poppy Andrews (7)
Hayes School, Paignton

Rubbish Collector

I have a driver and a loader.
I'm noisy and smelly.
I'm green and big.
I'll eat your rubbish and turn it into something else.
Dad works there.
I have big, black wheels.
What am I?

Answer: A bin wagon.

Dylan Hazlewood (7)
Hayes School, Paignton

Candy Magic

I am a magical creature
because I can do mysterious, magic tricks.
I am very rare, like a delicate diamond.
I am hard to find, like a rare ruby.
I am mostly pink.
I can be a kind beauty.
I have rosy red hair like your cheeks in sun.
What am I?

Answer: A unicorn.

Evie Tuffee (6)
Hextable Primary School, Hextable

Fast Reptile

I'm the only dinosaur that can open doors.
I have long toenails.
Like a cheetah, I run so fast you cannot see me.
I'm the size of a six-year-old boy.
I have teeth the size of pencils.
I can fight a triceratops.
What am I?

Answer: A raptor.

Maxwell Wilson (7)
Hextable Primary School, Hextable

Very Fluffy

I can be all different colours.
I fly in the morning sky.
I am as fluffy as a cloud floating up above us.
I am as colourful and as beautiful as a rainbow.
A bird sometimes loses me.
I am very good for tickling people.
What am I?

Answer: A feather.

Scarlet Larkham (7)
Hextable Primary School, Hextable

In The Sky

I am a fast flyer, like a bird in the sky.
I have wings like a pterodactyl.
I can carry passengers like a busy bus.
I can be as white as a piece of paper.
I am bigger than a house.
I fly in the blue sky like an eagle.
What am I?

Answer: A plane.

Joseph Gradley (7)
Hextable Primary School, Hextable

Useful Toy

I come in different sizes.
I am as colourful as a picture.
You might find me on the shelf.
I'm as round as a football.
I am useful.
I don't move by myself.
I spin round and round like a football.
What am I?

Answer: A globe.

Herbie Bishop (6)
Hextable Primary School, Hextable

Shiny

I am as bright as a firefly
sparkling in the night sky.
I'm as red as Santa's red suit.
I am as green as the grass
or as deep blue as the deep sea.
Pirates like me very much.
A lady might wear me.
What am I?

Answer: A gem.

Lennie Davey (7)
Hextable Primary School, Hextable

In The Mud

I am ginormous, like a dinosaur.
I pick things up with my naughty nose.
I am fluffy like a feather.
My eyes are as big as a house.
I have smooth, shiny eyes.
I like to bathe in the sticky, squelchy mud.
What am I?

Answer: An elephant.

Ava Stanton (7)
Hextable Primary School, Hextable

Foot Loose

I arrive in a box.
I come in all different sizes.
I tread on stuff a lot.
Something goes inside me.
I am stinky.
I come in all different colours.
Sometimes I am inside.
Sometimes I'm outside.
What am I?

Answer: A shoe.

Kian Stanley Waterton (6)
Hextable Primary School, Hextable

Shiny

I am as bright as a firefly.
I am as orange as a hot fire
and as green as the grass
and as yellow as a daffodil.
People wear me on their necks or arms.
Girls love me very much.
Jade is one of me.
What am I?

Answer: A gem.

Zachary Maddox Extance Vaughan (6)
Hextable Primary School, Hextable

Who Am I?

I have sparkly hair.
I live in a palace like a queen.
My crown is shiny and smooth.
My dress is flowing like the wind waving.
I have yellow hair like the bright sun.
I live with a handsome prince.
Who am I?

Answer: A princess.

Holly Way (6)

Hextable Primary School, Hextable

Bumpy All Over

I am as round as the sun.
I am as bumpy as the soil.
You can gently spin me on your bumpy finger.
I am very light for you to hold me.
You can carefully roll me about.
You can bounce me in your game.
What am I?

Answer: A ball.

Laila Frances Pruden (7)
Hextable Primary School, Hextable

Black And White

I am cheeky like a baboon.
I come out at midnight.
I am as fast as a cheetah.
I wear black and white stripes like a zebra.
I rob big banks with my gang of gangsters.
I'm put behind bars a lot.
Who am I?

Answer: A robber.

Jamie Martin Peters (7)
Hextable Primary School, Hextable

What Am I?

I have sparkling hair.
Its bright red, like the sun.
I have a scaly, bumpy tail.
I have a bright green shell house.
I live in the deep, dark sea.
I live with bright, colourful fishes.
What am I?

Answer: A mermaid.

Jessica Theobald (6)
Hextable Primary School, Hextable

What Am I?

I'm a hungry herbivore.
I am very stripy.
I have four legs like a cat.
I'm fluffy like a bouncing bunny.
I live in Africa in the boiling sun.
I am soft and cuddly like a teddy.
What am I?

Answer: A zebra.

Justin Rhys Webber (7)
Hextable Primary School, Hextable

What Am I?

I have people swimming in me.
I may have shiny shells under me.
I am blue like the beautiful sky.
I go *splish splash!*
Boats sail on me day and night.
Scary sharks live in me.
What am I?

Answer: *The sea.*

Ibukunoluwani Lawal (6)
Hextable Primary School, Hextable

Claws

I am very caring and curious.
I am as fluffy as a sheep.
My dinner is from the deep blue sea.
My ears are as pointy as a triangle.
I am as lazy as sloths.
I love to give hugs.
What am I?

Answer: A kitten.

Winter McCrae Caroline Jacob (7)
Hextable Primary School, Hextable

A Big Predator

I have a wife who is the queen.
I have hair to keep me warm in the jungle.
I am as handsome as your daddy.
I hunt down my prey.
My voice is loud.
I am the boss of the jungle.
What am I?

Answer: A lion.

Summer Rose Hartley (6)
Hextable Primary School, Hextable

High Up In The Sky

I am as bright as sunshine.
I come out at night.
I twinkle and dance in the sky.
I look tiny but I'm very big.
I shine brighter than a light.
My home is high in the sky.
What am I?

Answer: A star.

Charlotte Lily Warren (6)
Hextable Primary School, Hextable

What Am I?

I come in many different colours.
You'll find me in most houses.
I am pulled all the time.
I come with a pole.
My job is to keep the light away.
I come in any size.
What am I?

Answer: A curtain.

Skyla Tull (7)
Hextable Primary School, Hextable

Heavy, Heavy

I live in the dark blue sky.
I am as hard as a chestnut.
I am as round as a grey football.
I am very big and I live in the sky.
I can give you light when the sun shines on me.
What am I?

Answer: The moon.

Erin Davie (6)
Hextable Primary School, Hextable

What Am I?

I have a carrot nose.
My skin is as cold as ice.
I wear a top hat and a scarf.
Bunnies like to eat my nose.
My nose is a reindeer's favourite treat.
I get built.
What am I?

Answer: A snowman.

Charlotte Ann Hilton (6)
Hextable Primary School, Hextable

Go, Go Blosom

I grow in the summer.
I'm as soft as a piece of fluff.
I can shine in the sunlight.
I'm pretty as a butterfly.
I come in light colours.
I have soil around me.
What am I?

Answer: A flower.

Ruby Joy Diaz Jones (6)
Hextable Primary School, Hextable

My Best Friend

Children play with me.
I love to be hugged.
I love it when children dress me up.
Children like to sleep with me.
I come in all shapes and sizes.
People like me.
What am I?

Answer: A teddy bear.

Edmin Mamedova (6)
Hextable Primary School, Hextable

Dirty Everywhere

I can be all sizes.
I can be heavy and light.
I can be as round as the moon.
I am as round as a sphere.
I can be any colour.
You can hit me with a tennis racquet.
What am I?

Answer: A ball.

Jake Ray (7)
Hextable Primary School, Hextable

Shining In The Dark

I live on a desert island.
I am bored with no company.
I am as tall as a tree.
I am surrounded by the sea.
I shine like the stars.
I help to guide boats.
What am I?

Answer: A lighthouse.

Hazel O'Hara (7)
Hextable Primary School, Hextable

What Am I?

I can be many colours, like red, orange or green.
I can be sharp, like a pencil.
I can be light or dark.
You can hold me in your hand.
I can make your picture.
What am I?

Answer: A crayon.

Willow Jones-Harvey (6)
Hextable Primary School, Hextable

Slitherer

I am as long as an elephant's trunk.
I'm as slimy as a piece of goo.
I'm as long as a crocodile.
I'm very sly.
I'm as stripy as a zebra.
What am I?

Answer: A python.

Angus Crawford Bunch (7)
Hextable Primary School, Hextable

What Am I?

I am thick and hard like the moon.
I am as round as the moon.
I am as bouncy as a kangaroo.
I am soft on my bright outside.
I am hard and dark inside.
What am I?

Answer: A tennis ball.

Grace Eleanor Diaz Jones (6)
Hextable Primary School, Hextable

Rolling In The Mud

I am very pink like a worm.
When I am clean I am smooth like a snake.
I have a curly tail like a lizard.
I live on the farm.
I always roll around in the mud.
What am I?

Answer: A pig.

Daniela Bayliss (7)
Hextable Primary School, Hextable

Colour Fly

I love to fly fast.
I come from Australia.
I am colourful.
I am shaped like a half of the moon.
I go very fast and come back.
I fly in the air.
What am I?

Answer: A boomerang.

Peony Collins (7)
Hextable Primary School, Hextable

Shiny

I am as bright as a firefly sparkling in the night sky.
I am as hot as a fire and as yellow as a dandelion.
I am as green as grass.
Pirates like me very much.
What am I?

Answer: A gem.

Ethan O'Malley (7)
Hextable Primary School, Hextable

My Buddy

I come in different sizes.
I am soft and enjoy a cuddle.
I am an animal.
You might find me everywhere.
I come in different colours.
I am a pet.
What am I?

Answer: A dog.

Sydney Payne (6)
Hextable Primary School, Hextable

Midnight

People are scared of me.
I am cute and fluffy.
I am not a pet!
I am big and black.
I eat insects and bugs.
I am nocturnal.
I am a mammal.
What am I?

Answer: A bat.

Natalie Adrianova (7)
Hextable Primary School, Hextable

Stripy

I am black and white.
I live at the zoo.
I like eating grass.
My mane is furry and cuddly.
My mane is black and white as well.
I am stripy.
What am I?

Answer: A zebra.

Jessica Hawkett (7)
Hextable Primary School, Hextable

Teatime Treat

I am as crunchy as a carrot.
I am brown, like mud.
I am as yummy as Coca-Cola.
You dip me in your tea.
I am a melty, tasty treat.
What am I?

Answer: A Bourbon biscuit.

Louie Robb (6)
Hextable Primary School, Hextable

A Day At The Beach

I live at the beach.
I have feathery wings.
I can fly in the sky.
I have a sharp beak to eat with.
I eat seafood.
I squawk loudly.
What am I?

Answer: A seagull.

Pearl O'Connor (7)
Hextable Primary School, Hextable

Teatime Treat

I am as crunchy as a carrot.
I am as yummy as chocolate.
I am brown, like mud.
You can dip me in your tea.
I am a melty treat.
What am I?

Answer: A Bourbon biscuit.

Evelyn Ava Hilden (6)
Hextable Primary School, Hextable

What Am I?

I need the sun to help me grow.
I need lots of food, also water.
You might find me outside.
I smell lovely.
I am all shapes and sizes.
What am I?

Answer: A flower.

Jessica Joyce Ellis (6)
Hextable Primary School, Hextable

Fluffy

I'm fluffy and green as a leaf.
A soft and bendy flyer.
I'm as fluffy as a rabbit's tail.
Birds fly with me to keep them warm.
What am I?

Answer: A feather.

Skye Winnie Hunt-McCauley (7)
Hextable Primary School, Hextable

Plumbing Problems

People twist me all the time.
I can be hot and cold.
You might use me at school.
I can be shiny.
Sometimes I am noisy.
I am drippy.
What am I?

Answer: A tap.

Lilia Scarlett Hurst (7)
Hextable Primary School, Hextable

Hoppity Hop

I am soft to touch.
I love to eat carrots.
I always hop around.
I wiggle my nose.
You can have me as a pet.
I am very fluffy.
What am I?

Answer: A rabbit.

Alice Brabbs Williams (6)
Hextable Primary School, Hextable

Under The Sea

I live under the sea.
I am blue.
I am very flat.
I like to swim and sleep.
I like to sting people.
My face is on my tummy.
What am I?

Answer: A stingray.

Ryan Dwight (7)
Hextable Primary School, Hextable

Down Under

I come from Australia.
I am shaped like a banana.
People throw me but I always come back.
I can be different sizes and colours.
What am I?

Answer: A boomerang.

Kayla Pearl Rosette Rendell (6)
Hextable Primary School, Hextable

Lightning Blaze

I am furry.
I have a white tail.
I run as fast as I can.
I eat grass.
I work out and jog on the track.
I pull a cart.
What am I?

Answer: A horse.

Joseph Ripley (6)
Hextable Primary School, Hextable

My Tweety Pie

I can be a copycat.
I am as colourful as a rainbow.
I fly in the sky.
My coat is made from feathers.
I am an animal.
What am I?

Answer: A parrot.

Amelie Thorne (6)
Hextable Primary School, Hextable

What Am I?

I am crunchy as a carrot.
I am as yummy as chocolate.
You can dip me in your tea.
I am a melty, tasty treat.
What am I?

Answer: A Bourbon biscuit.

Ruby Marsh (6)
Hextable Primary School, Hextable

Rest Your Head

You might find me on a bed.
You might find me on a sofa.
I come in any colour.
You can sleep with me.
What am I?

Answer: A pillow.

Oliver Murphy (6)
Hextable Primary School, Hextable

The Very Good Goalkeeper

I play football.
I like using my hands.
I am a goalkeeper.
I am very good.
I play for Manchester United.
I love playing football.
I play for an international team.
Who am I?

Answer: David de Gea Quintana.

Frankie Dadds (7)
Oasis Academy New Oak, Hengrove

Playing Object

I can be played with.
I am electric.
I can be charged up.
I am flat.
I'm not a pad that a frog can sit on.
I have lots of games on me.
My enormous cover protects me.
What am I?

Answer: An iPad.

Layla Charkaoui (7)
Oasis Academy New Oak, Hengrove

The Flying Help

I am super fast.
I am really big.
I have a lot of work.
I help a lot of people.
I come in some emergencies.
I am sometimes busy.
What am I?

Answer: The Great Western Air Ambulance.

Megan Jones (7)
Oasis Academy New Oak, Hengrove

The Great Defender

I am very creative.
I have blonde hair.
I have lots of friends.
I am a brilliant left back.
I can play in midfield.
I am a good Bristol City player.
Who am I?

Answer: Joe Bryan.

Ethan Monks (7)
Oasis Academy New Oak, Hengrove

A Cheeky Creature

I eat delicious bananas.
I swing around on trees.
I am very naughty.
I am extremely funny.
I am curious and adventurous.
I'm like a gorilla.
What am I?

Answer: A monkey.

Summer-Jade Phillips (6)
Oasis Academy New Oak, Hengrove

The Magic Legend

I'm a legend.
I'm magical.
I don't get seen often.
I am very clever.
I am sparkly.
I have something sharp on my head.
What am I?

Answer: A unicorn.

Jessica Jones (7)
Oasis Academy New Oak, Hengrove

Little Babies

They are cold.
There are lots of them.
They have orange beaks and orange feet.
They are cute!
Sometimes they fight over babies.
What are they?

Answer: Penguins.

Leila Styles (7)
Oasis Academy New Oak, Hengrove

What Am I?

I have a screen.
I have letters.
You can go on Paint.
You can go on Notepad.
You can type on me.
You can go on Minesweeper.
What am I?

Answer: A laptop.

Alicia Mae Dennis (7)
Oasis Academy New Oak, Hengrove

Attack

It is scary.
It is in a movie.
It can swim.
It likes to find fish.
It has sharp teeth.
It can camouflage really fast.
What is it?

Answer: A shark.

Caitlin Avril Stutt (7)
Oasis Academy New Oak, Hengrove

A Little Snow Creature

I live in the snow.
I'm black.
I am cute.
I snuggle with my family.
I waddle.
I sometimes live on mountains.
What am I?

Answer: A penguin.

Isabella Nelson (7)
Oasis Academy New Oak, Hengrove

Fierce Feline

I love playing in water.
I live in India.
I am a predator.
I have stripes.
I can pounce.
I have sharp teeth.
What am I?

Answer: A tiger.

Masie Cook (7)
Oasis Academy New Oak, Hengrove

Shark Attack

I am black.
I am an animal.
I am a sea creature.
I have sharp teeth.
I eat fish.
I can breathe underwater.
What am I?

Answer: A shark.

Ollie Robinson (7)
Oasis Academy New Oak, Hengrove

Predator

I was the biggest predator a long time ago.
I have a spine on my back.
I go in the water.
I catch a lot of fish.
I have a big mouth like a crocodile.
I'm really dangerous!
What am I?

Answer: A spinosaurus.

Callum Humphrey (7)
Ravenswood School, Nailsea

Dinosaur Trouble

I am one of the two most fierce dinosaurs ever.
My vicious teeth can chomp through nearly anything.
I am one of the smallest carnivores in the dinosaur family.
My name means 'horned lizard'.
I am about three car lengths long.
I weigh as much as a brown bear.
What am I?

Answer: A ceratosaurus.

Alex Taylor (7)
Rookwood School, Andover

Lovely Friend

I am a pet and I live in a house.
I'm very jumpy when I play.
I sometimes growl when you try to get my toys.
I come in different colours.
I can have a wet or dry nose.
I chase cats.
What am I?

Answer: A dog.

Anita Mcgleish (6)
Rookwood School, Andover

Legs

I have a lot of legs.
I come in a lot of different colours.
I am quite small but sometimes I can be big.
I live in soil.
I eat insects.
My predators are birds, toads and shrews.
What am I?

Answer: A centipede.

Hugo Lockhart-Mirams (7)
Rookwood School, Andover

Big And Green

You will find me on a farm.
I have two big wheels and two little wheels.
I am green.
I am very useful on a farm.
I can pull heavy things.
I need a driver.
What am I?

Answer: A tractor.

George Rooke (7)
Rookwood School, Andover

Juicy And Yummy

I am red with seeds all over.
I have a stalk with leaves around.
I am juicy and yummy.
I grow on a farm.
People like to eat me.
I get sold in the shop.
What am I?

Answer: A strawberry.

Samantha Crompton (7)
Rookwood School, Andover

Stomping

I have sharp horns.
I eat leaves.
I lived a long time ago.
I come in different colours.
I have a big crest on my head.
I like stomping around.
What am I?

Answer: A triceratops.

Isabelle Emma Rowland (6)
Rookwood School, Andover

Attack

I am scary and orange.
I have a wet, black nose.
I eat chickens and rabbits.
I live in the forest.
I have a fluffy tail.
I am shy sometimes.
What am I?

Answer: A fox.

Harry Brewer (7)
Rookwood School, Andover

Keytastic

I am very big.
I have lots of keys.
I have three pedals.
Lots of people press my keys.
Music comes out of me.
I love kids playing on me.
What am I?

Answer: A piano.

Megan Light (7)
Rookwood School, Andover

Underwater

I am very stretchy.
I live in the ocean.
I spray ink if I am frightened.
I am bright red.
I have lots of legs.
I eat fish and crabs.
What am I?

Answer: An octopus.

Theo Wickens (7)
Rookwood School, Andover

Serving

I work in a restaurant.
I am always happy.
I serve food and drink.
I give out bills.
I tidy up the mess that the customers make.
I take orders for food and drink.
I'm helpful to people.
I tell cooks what people want
for their dinner, breakfast and tea.
Who am I?

Answer: A waitress.

Bella Dunn (7)
Severn Beach Primary School, Severn Beach

Classroom Creatures

They're nice and kind
and they'll help expand your mind.
They can be strict
if your work is not ticked.
You can't find them in the zoo
but they'll help you solve two plus two.
They love to drink tea
and they'll help you and me.
Who are they?

Answer: Teachers.

Xanthe Larner (7)
Severn Beach Primary School, Severn Beach

Goo-Goo

I like to crawl
and I sometimes cry.
I always want milk
and I don't know why.
I laugh, I babble
and I like to play.
I cuddle my mummy
and nap in the day.
Who am I?

Answer: A baby.

John Corcoran (6)
Severn Beach Primary School, Severn Beach

Furry Magic

I have fluffy ears.
I'm a vegetarian.
I have a big marshmallowy tail.
I live in a burrow.
I have a furry coat.
You can pull me out of a hat.
What am I?

Answer: A rabbit.

Sam Slocombe (5)

Severn Beach Primary School, Severn Beach

Pet Shop

I am fluffy.
Sometimes I am a bit cheeky.
I have a black nose.
I have brown eyes.
People feed me.
I love it when they feed me.
I stand on four feet.
I run away.
You can have me for a pet.
I am part of the wolf family.
I chase cats.
People adore me.
What am I?

Answer: A dog.

Delilah Weale (6)
Shebbear College, Shebbear

Yummy

I smell them sometimes
Although I don't have them very much.
I like them.
They come from a shop.
They are yellow and I think they are my favourite.
I like them with a burger.
What are they?

Answer: Chips.

Lila-Mai McHugh (7)
Shebbear College, Shebbear

Party

It can be rainbow colours.
You can eat it.
It doesn't go creamy.
I like the red one.
Some people like it with ice cream.
It wobbles.
What is it?

Answer: Jelly.

Emma Clewley (6)
Shebbear College, Shebbear

Squirty And Squashy

You can buy us in a shop.
We are in a basket.
We are lots of different colours.
We are healthy.
We are juicy.
Lots of us grow on trees.
What are we?

Answer: Fruit.

Elizabeth McEwan (6)
Shebbear College, Shebbear

Mr Juicy

You can eat me.
I am juicy.
I am red and small.
There are lots of me.
I have green on top.
I am great to eat in the summer.
What am I?

Answer: A strawberry.

James Clewley (7)
Shebbear College, Shebbear

Fluffy

I don't make a noise.
I feel fluffy.
I have a white face.
I have black ears.
I have claws.
I eat bamboo.
What am I?

Answer: A panda.

Dixie-Belle Whatling (6)
Shebbear College, Shebbear

Mr Stamp

I have a big tail.
I sound very noisy.
I live in the zoo.
I eat straw.
I feel strong.
I like stamping.
What am I?

Answer: An elephant.

Ashton James Saltmarsh (7)
Shebbear College, Shebbear

Cheeky

You can find me in a tree.
I am cheeky.
I am brown.
I have a tail.
I eat yellow food.
I swing on vines.
What am I?

Answer: A monkey.

Tyler Douglas (6)
Shebbear College, Shebbear

Cheeky Chimps

I live in the rainforest.
I have a tail.
I am brown.
I am cheeky.
I swing in trees.
I like bananas.
What am I?

Answer: A monkey.

Carter Singleton (7)
Shebbear College, Shebbear

Dangerous

I am fluffy.
I eat meat.
I prey on other animals.
I am dangerous.
I am the king of the cats.
What am I?

Answer: A lion.

James Winkworth (6)
Shebbear College, Shebbear

Scrumptious

I am round.
You can eat me.
I smell delicious.
I am covered in cheese.
What am I?

Answer: A pizza.

Sonny-Beau Whatling (5)
Shebbear College, Shebbear

Long Numbers

I am long, like a stick.
You will use me at school and at home.
There are numbers on me.
I begin with an R and end with an R.
I am long.
I am short.
I can snap easily.
I am made out of plastic or wood.
I am straight and I have lines.
What am I?

Answer: A ruler.

Libby Nicholson (7)
Sheet Primary School, Sheet

Shine

I hide by day, I shine at night.
People look up at me and think I'm cheese.
I am round, like a sphere.
People have walked on me.
Sometimes you can see all of me,
Sometimes you can see half of me.
I have a flag on top of me.
What am I?

Answer: The moon.

Evie Greenwood (7)
Sheet Primary School, Sheet

Hard As Nails

I'm bumpy, rough and hard.
Shells sometimes make homes on me.
I am as hard as the moon.
I live on the beach with the sea creatures.
I could be red.
If it's high tide, I sometimes get covered with sea.
What am I?

Answer: A rock.

Emily Law (6)
Sheet Primary School, Sheet

The Bright Colours

My colours are bright.
Can you guess what I am?
My colours shine in the sun and rain.
I am red, orange, yellow, blue, green
And purple in an arch.
Get to my end and find a pot of gold.
What am I?

Answer: A rainbow.

Iris Lawson-McKittrick (6)
Sheet Primary School, Sheet

The Flying Thing

I can fly.
I can breathe fire hotter than the sun.
I'm redder than a red pen.
Sometimes knights like me.
I'm very scaly.
I am so big.
I begin with the letter D.
What am I?

Answer: A dragon.

Riley Heighes (7)
Sheet Primary School, Sheet

The Bright Colours

My colours are light, bright,
Beautiful, colourful and sparkly.
People like to see me.
You only see me when the rain
And sun are out.
You find treasure at the end of me.
What am I?

Answer: A rainbow.

Daisy Swanton (6)
Sheet Primary School, Sheet

Flying Delivery

I pull a heavy load full of exciting things.
I have antlers.
I fly.
My red nose shines like the sun.
I carry a jolly man who wears red.
I like Christmas.
What am I?

Answer: A reindeer.

Josh Dodson (7)
Sheet Primary School, Sheet

What Am I?

You will see my colours sometimes.
You will find gold at the end of me.
I am as beautiful as can be.
Everyone likes to see me.
I am a half circle.
What am I?

Answer: A rainbow.

Finley Griffiths (6)
Sheet Primary School, Sheet

Hard Shell

I live in America.
I begin with the letter T.
I have brown and maroon on my shell.
I swim in swamps.
I have teeth.
I am small.
What am I?

Answer: A terrapin.

James (7)
Sheet Primary School, Sheet

Big Thing

It can climb.
It is cute.
It is black and white.
Some hair is pink.
Definitely fun.
Definitely cuddly.
It eats bamboo.
What is it?

Answer: A panda.

Emily Morrill (6)
Sheet Primary School, Sheet

Colours

Lovely colours in the sky.
Different colours.
It is in the sky.
It has brilliant colours.
People like to see it.
What is it?

Answer: A rainbow.

Isabel Thomas (5)
Sheet Primary School, Sheet

What Am I?

I have a lead.
I have pink skin.
I have a fluffy tail and a nose.
I sit on shoulders.
I eat Felix tuna.
What am I?

Answer: A cat.

Theo Carter (7)
Sheet Primary School, Sheet

Sparkly

I am shiny.
I am a type of rock.
I am rare.
I am valuable.
I can be in jewellery like a ring.
What am I?

Answer: A sapphire.

Oliver Burgess (7)
Sheet Primary School, Sheet

Colourful

I have lovely colours in the sky.
I look beautiful in the sun.
I have lovely colours in a semi-circle.
What am I?

Answer: A rainbow.

Eva Greenslade (5)
Sheet Primary School, Sheet

Wings

I am big.
I can breathe fire.
I have a tail.
I have big teeth.
What am I?

Answer: A dragon.

Aidan Busuttil (5)
Sheet Primary School, Sheet

Rainbow Power

I have long hair like Rapunzel.
I am so cute.
What a lovely sparkling horn I've got!
I am popular because I am amazing.
I am not real, but I was real.
Wow! I can come in any colour I like.
How kind and honest I am.
What am I?

Answer: A unicorn.

Lola Williams (7)
St Martin's Garden Primary School, Odd Down

Golden Sparkle

I come in lots of different colours.
I am gold.
I can sparkle in the sun a little.
I'm a gem.
I've been found under the ground.
I am amazing because I am pretty.
Most people like to look at me.
What am I?

Answer: Topaz.

Taheena Chowdhury (7)
St Martin's Garden Primary School, Odd Down

The Black Rock

I am treasure for a pirate.
If you buy me it will cost you an amazing £1,000,000.
I'm a rare mineral.
I'm found very deep underground.
People wear me on a golden ring.
What am I?

Answer: A diamond.

Jacob David Lewis (6)
St Martin's Garden Primary School, Odd Down

I'm A Flyer

I can talk and squawk
There are a lot of me
A cage can be my home
Also, I like staying on a lot of shoulders
I can fly to different places
What a beautiful creature I am
What am I?

Answer: A parrot.

Aimee Schofield (7)
St Martin's Garden Primary School, Odd Down

Wand

My wand is magic.
My cat is as ginger as a fox.
My hat is a magic hat and it is brown.
I have a wand and a ginger cat and a pot.
I make spells and I can turn you into a frog.
What am I?

Answer: A wizard.

Erin Sherwood (6)
St Martin's Garden Primary School, Odd Down

Puzzler!

I am six-faced
I am a 3D shape
I am multicoloured
You have to solve me
I am hard to solve
I come on a triangle-shaped stand
What sharp verticals I have
What am I?

Answer: A Rubik's cube.

Ashton Morrissey-Hoskin (7)
St Martin's Garden Primary School, Odd Down

The Hot Fire

I can fly so high like a bird in the sky.
I can breathe hot fire, as hot as toast.
I'm very good at flying.
My fire is orange.
I am colourful.
I am very big.
What am I?

Answer: A dragon.

Kyle Martin (7)
St Martin's Garden Primary School, Odd Down

Sparkle Power

I come in lots of different colours.
I am sparkly and shiny.
I come from underground.
You can wear me.
I am very precious.
I can be big or small.
What am I?

Answer: A sapphire.

Heather Jade Bean (7)
St Martin's Garden Primary School, Odd Down

The Last Coach

I have blue and red coaches.
My tender has lots of coal.
I'm as fast as a Jaguar.
How big am I?
My boiler is in the middle of my body.
What am I?

Answer: A train.

Jakub Chelstowski (7)
St Martin's Garden Primary School, Odd Down

My Furry Friend

When I am happy, I purr.
I'm very fluffy.
Mind out! I might scratch like a lion.
We all have nine lives.
I love to chase scared mice.
What am I?

Answer: A cat.

Nyah Quinnell-Reid (7)
St Martin's Garden Primary School, Odd Down

Furball

I eat bamboo.
I come from China.
I am sleepy.
I am a large animal.
I have black and white fur.
I am endangered.
I am cute.
What am I?

Answer: A panda.

Natalie Pranczuk-Doubrouska (7)
St Martin's Garden Primary School, Odd Down

Roxy

I have four legs.
My nose is wet like the rain.
I go on a lead.
I have very sharp teeth.
I can lick you with my long, pink tongue.
What am I?

Answer: A dog.

Ashley Powell (7)
St Martin's Garden Primary School, Odd Down

My Pedal Friend

I have wheels as round as a football.
I have a bell so people can get out of my way.
I have a chain so the back wheels can go.
What am I?

Answer: A bike.

Jack White (6)
St Martin's Garden Primary School, Odd Down

The Web Power

I climb on a web.
Small as a ladybird.
I'm as black as the night.
I have sharp teeth.
I live in dark places.
What am I?

Answer: A spider.

Wojciech Cejrowski (6)
St Martin's Garden Primary School, Odd Down

Rainbow Power

It has a small horn.
It has a long rainbow tail.
It is rainbow-coloured.
It is not real.
It is magic.
What is it?

Answer: A rainbow unicorn.

Summer Lewis (6)
St Martin's Garden Primary School, Odd Down

Fire Friend

I can burn the forest.
I can be scary.
I have a pointed tail.
I am strong.
I am humongous!
What am I?

Answer: A dragon.

Leland Jones (6)
St Martin's Garden Primary School, Odd Down

The Fast Machine

I go forty to fifty miles an hour!
I am mega fast.
I am used for good touring.
I have four wheels.
What am I?

Answer: A car.

Leon Ricketts (6)
St Martin's Garden Primary School, Odd Down

Who Am I?

My loyal friend has ginger hair.
I have a bossy friend.
I have a scar like a lightning bolt that could zap you to death.
I fly around the dangerous field on my trusty broomstick.
I go around and solve mysteries with my trusty and silly friends.
I like to catch Golden Snitches.
I'm always bossed around by my friend.
I've seen lots of wizards.
Who am I?

Answer: Harry Potter.

Brooke Franklin (7)
Stoke Park Primary School, Lockleaze

The Screwdriver

I will zap you to death with my secret weapon.
I will regenerate like a chameleon changing colour.
I can go anywhere in my bright blue box,
that's bigger on the inside than the outside.
I am faster than ever.
I will defeat all those mean things.
My screwdriver will tell you who I am.
Who am I?

Answer: The Doctor.

Bayley Drew (6)
Stoke Park Primary School, Lockleaze

The Ring Collector

I am fast, like a zooming cheetah,
I am a hedgehog with hedgehog friends
that work together to defeat mean, awful
bad guys.
I collect golden, shiny rings with my friends,
all the way to the mean, awful bad guys.
I have pointy spikes on my head.
Who am I?

Answer: Sonic.

Archie Neale (7)
Stoke Park Primary School, Lockleaze

Roger

I always help people and we do it.
My shield is impossible to break.
I always fight villains with my mighty shield.
I run fast and I can throw my shield.
It's impossible to kill me.
Who am I?

Answer: Captain America.

Harvey Mark Bee's (6)
Stoke Park Primary School, Lockleaze

Lady Lamp

I wear a black and white dress.
I have a lamp with glistening lights.
I have a rope on my head.
I was in the war.
I have pink cheeks.
I am famous and come from a rich family.
Who am I?

Answer: Florence Nightingale.

Evie Butt (6)
Stoke Park Primary School, Lockleaze

Magic Mystery

I have a pet that can fly
and I have a magic broomstick.
I always had a mystery.
I fly around the field.
I like catching Golden Snitches.
I am fast and smarter than a bird.
Who am I?

Answer: Harry Potter.

Mohammed Elsadig Yagoeb (6)
Stoke Park Primary School, Lockleaze

Top Hat Man

I made beautiful bridges.
I made a wonderful ship as big as a giant.
I wore a hat, a top hat.
I wore a smart suit.
I am not alive anymore.
Who am I?

Answer: Brunel.

Taija Louise Allen (6)
Stoke Park Primary School, Lockleaze

What Am I?

I have a big, hairy mane.
I roam the African wild.
I hunt for my prey.
I have fearsome roars.
I am the king of the jungle.
What am I?

Answer: A lion guard.

Hassan Omar (7)
Stoke Park Primary School, Lockleaze

Enormous Growls

I have a big, hairy mane.
I roam the African wild.
I hunt for my prey.
I have fearsome roars.
I am the king of the jungle.
What am I?

Answer: A lion.

Ryan Collins (6)
Stoke Park Primary School, Lockleaze

Top Hat Man

I made beautiful bridges as long as a snake.
I made a wonderful ship as huge as a giant.
I had a top hat.
I am no longer alive.
Who am I?

Answer: Brunel.

Milosz Siecinski (7)
Stoke Park Primary School, Lockleaze

The Famous Lady

I speak positively.
I wear something sparkly.
I sit on a throne.
I am Royal.
People come to visit me.
Who am I?

Answer: Queen Elizabeth II.

Layla Toogood (6)
Stoke Park Primary School, Lockleaze

The Posh Lady

I am famous.
I wear something that is sparkly.
I had a Bible.
I wear jewels.
I am from a rich family.
Who am I?

Answer: Queen Victoria.

Minnie Jamelia Manu Edkins (7)
Stoke Park Primary School, Lockleaze

Top Hat Man

I made beautiful bridges as long as a snake.
I made a wonderful ship as big as a mountain.
I'm no longer alive.
Who am I?

Answer: Brunel.

Micah Ogbu (7)
Stoke Park Primary School, Lockleaze

Top Hat Man

I made beautiful bridges as long as a snake.
I made a wonderful ship as big as a giant.
My hat is black as coal.
Who am I?

Answer: Brunel.

Elly Underwood (6)
Stoke Park Primary School, Lockleaze

Top Hat Man

I made a huge, beautiful bridge
I made a wonderful ship
I wore a black top hat
I am not alive.
Who am I?

Answer: Brunel.

Brianne Georgina Bond (6)
Stoke Park Primary School, Lockleaze

Top Hat Man

I love to build bridges and boats.
I am an engineer.
I was famous.
Who am I?

Answer: Brunel.

Filip Nogawka (6)
Stoke Park Primary School, Lockleaze

Spooky Space

I am like a person that sucks up juice
but I'm in space.
I sound silent.
I look like black space.
I suck up anything that comes near.
I come when a star explodes.
No one can touch me!
What am I?

Answer: A black hole.

Vihaan Saraiya (7)
The Ursuline Preparatory School, Ilford

A Relaxing Area

It is a really relaxing place.
There are a lot of chairs inside of it.
It is next to the kitchen.
It is a huge place.
It also has some sofas.
It has a fireplace.
What is this place?

Answer: A living room.

Ezaan Shaikh (6)
The Ursuline Preparatory School, Ilford

Clever Clogs!

I need electricity.
I have buttons.
People play games on me.
I am noisy.
People like me.
I can't move.
I'm full of knowledge.
What am I?

Answer: A computer.

Swayam Sinha (6)
The Ursuline Preparatory School, Ilford

What Is Black And Hangs Upside Down?

It hangs upside down.
It flies at night.
It likes the dark.
It can't see very well.
It is a nocturnal animal.
It is very good at hearing.
What is it?

Answer: A bat.

Aniyah Akram (6)
The Ursuline Preparatory School, Ilford

What Am I?

I go around on missions.
I have gadgets.
I'm cool.
I'm rude.
I swing around on my gun rope.
I'm in stealth mode.
What am I?

Answer: A spy.

Shemilore Aderugbo (7)
The Ursuline Preparatory School, Ilford

What Is It?

It is wet.
A coat keeps us warm on this kind of day.
It makes you wet.
You get cold by it.
It stops you from going to school.
What is it?

Answer: Rain.

Kayla Olatunji (6)
The Ursuline Preparatory School, Ilford

What Am I?

I rhyme with torn.
I love rainbows.
I love gold.
I love money.
You can't catch me.
I'm not real.
What am I?

Answer: A leprechaun.

Kayla Gadiagellan (6)
The Ursuline Preparatory School, Ilford

What Am I?

You can't touch me.
I come when it rains.
I have seven colours.
I am bright.
What am I?

Answer: A rainbow.

Larelle Amanda Burnett (7)
The Ursuline Preparatory School, Ilford

What Am I?

I have a mane.
I am very loud.
I make a roar.
I am a carnivore!
What am I?

Answer: A lion.

Tiffany Marria Azumah (6)
The Ursuline Preparatory School, Ilford

YoungWriters
Est.1991

YOUNG WRITERS INFORMATION

We hope you have enjoyed reading this book – and that you will continue to in the coming years.

If you're a young writer who enjoys reading and creative writing, or the parent of an enthusiastic poet or story writer, do visit our website **www.youngwriters.co.uk**. Here you will find free competitions, workshops and games, as well as recommended reads, a poetry glossary and our blog.

If you would like to order further copies of this book, or any of our other titles, then please give us a call or visit **www.youngwriters.co.uk**.

Young Writers
Remus House
Coltsfoot Drive
Peterborough
PE2 9BF
(01733) 890066
info@youngwriters.co.uk